AUDIO
ACCESS
INCLUDED

PLAYBACK+
Speed • Pitch • Balance • Loop

IRISH FAVORITES

CONTENTS

T0088507

To access audio visit:
www.halleonard.com/mylibrary
Enter Code
4207-6074-3669-0919

ISBN 978-1-4234-9521-5

7777 W. BLUEMOUND RD. P.O. BOX 13819 MILWAUKEE, WI 53213

Visit Hal Leonard Online at
www.halleonard.com

BELIEVE ME, IF ALL THOSE
ENDEARING YOUNG CHARMS

FLUTE

Words and Music by
THOMAS MOORE

THE BELLS OF ST. MARY'S

Flute

Words by DOUGLAS FURBER
Music by A. EMMETT ADAMS

BLACK VELVET BAND

FLUTE

Traditional

BRENNAN ON THE MOOR

FLUTE

Traditional

COCKLES AND MUSSELS
(Molly Malone)

FLUTE

Traditional

THE CROPPY BOY

FLUTE

18th Century Irish Folksong

DANNY BOY

Words by FREDERICK EDWARD WEATHERLY
Traditional Irish Folk Melody

Flute

EASY AND SLOW

FLUTE

Traditional

THE FOGGY DEW

FLUTE

Traditional

GREEN GROW THE RUSHES, O

FLUTE

Traditional

THE HUMOUR IS ON ME NOW

FLUTE

Traditional

I ONCE LOVED A LASS

FLUTE

Traditional

I'LL TAKE YOU HOME AGAIN, KATHLEEN

FLUTE

Words and Music by
THOMAS WESTENDORF

I'LL TELL ME MA

FLUTE

Traditional

THE IRISH ROVER

FLUTE

Traditional

THE JOLLY BEGGARMAN

FLUTE

Traditional

THE LITTLE BEGGARMAN

FLUTE

Traditional

MacNAMARA'S BAND

Words by JOHN J. STAMFORD
Music by SHAMUS O'CONNOR

MINSTREL BOY

FLUTE

Traditional

MY WILD IRISH ROSE

Words and Music by
CHAUNCEY OLCOTT

Flute

A NATION ONCE AGAIN

FLUTE

Words and Music by
THOMAS DAVIS

THE OLD ORANGE FLUTE

FLUTE

Traditional

THE PATRIOT GAME

FLUTE

Traditional

RED IS THE ROSE

FLUTE

Irish Folksong

THE RISING OF THE MOON

FLUTE

Traditional

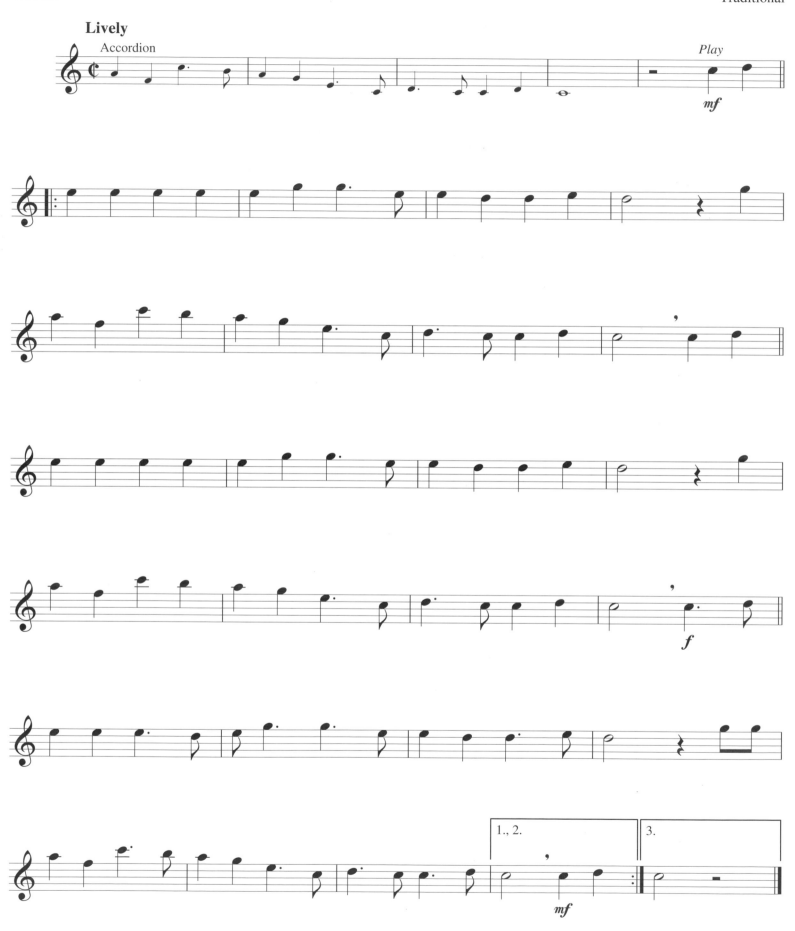

THE ROSE OF TRALEE

Words by C. MORDAUNT SPENCER
Music by CHARLES W. GLOVER

FLUTE

TOO-RA-LOO-RA-LOO-RAL
(That's an Irish Lullabye)

FLUTE

Words and Music by
JAMES R. SHANNON

THE WEARING OF THE GREEN

FLUTE

18th Century Irish Folksong

WHEN IRISH EYES ARE SMILING

FLUTE

Words by CHAUNCEY OLCOTT
and GEORGE GRAFF, JR.
Music by ERNEST R. BALL

THE WILD COLONIAL BOY

FLUTE

Traditional

WILD ROVER

FLUTE

Traditional